W9-ANN-405

International Food Library

FOOD IN
GREECE

International Food Library

FOOD IN
GREECE

text by
Nancy Loewen

recipes compiled by
Judith A. Ahlstrom

Rourke Publications, Inc.
Vero Beach, Florida 32964

Library of Congress Cataloging-in-Publication Data

Loewen, Nancy, 1964-
   Food in Greece / by Nancy Loewen
     p. cm. — (International food library)
   Includes index.
   Summary: Describes the food products, cooking and eating customs,
and festivals of Greece.
   ISBN 0-86625-348-3
   1. Cookery, Greek—Juvenile literature.   2. Greece—Social life
and customs—Juvenile literature. [1. Cookery, Greek. 2. Greece—
Social life and customs.] I. Title. II. Series.
TX723.5.G8L64   1991
641.59495—dc20   90-21272
                                  CIP

PRINTED IN THE USA   AC

CONTENTS

AN INTRODUCTION TO GREECE

At dusk, the people of Athens head outdoors for their traditional evening stroll. They exchange gossip with family and friends, or debate politics with their neighbors. Some folks stop to enjoy a glass of wine at one of the many outdoor cafés lining the sidewalks. The sprawling city of Athens becomes a maze of lights and conversations.

From a rocky hillside within the city, the ruins of the Acropolis seem to watch over the evening's activities. The stately columns of the Parthenon glow eerily in the fading light. The many stone sculptures seem to come to life. The Acropolis is an enduring reminder of an ancient and glorious civilization.

From the earliest times, Greece has been a land of
myth, beauty, and strength. It was here, about 2,500
years ago, that Western civilization first began to take
shape. The ideas of the ancient Greek philosophers,
scientists, playwrights, artists, and athletes are still
affecting Western culture today.

Greece is located on the Mediterranean Sea in southern
Europe. It includes nearly 3,000 islands, but only 169
of these islands are inhabited by people. Crete is the
largest and best-known island.

Greece is a mountainous country, and most of the land
is very rocky. The climate is similar to that of other
Mediterranean countries—winters are usually wet
and mild, and summers are hot, sunny, and dry.

Greece has a population of about 10 million. Nearly 40
percent of the people live in the metropolitan area of
Athens, which is also the capital city. Athens is named
for Athena, the goddess of wisdom. Thessaloniki and
Patras are other large cities in Greece.

7

ANCIENT GREECE

Even though they shared a common culture, the early Greeks were not united as one nation. Beginning in the 700's B.C., city-states emerged as the unit of government. They consisted of a city and the surrounding villages and farmland. Each city had a fortified hill, called an *acropolis*; and an *agora*, or public square. The biggest city-states were Athens and Sparta. Other important city-states were Corinth, Argos, and Thebes.

During the 500's B.C., Athens and some other city-states established the first democracies. All citizens could vote, hold political office, and serve on a jury. Citizenship itself, however, was very limited. Women could not vote or hold office, nor could slaves or foreigners. In addition, many people were too poor to take part in their government—they couldn't spare any time away from their work.

The Parthenon was built as a temple to Athena, goddess of wisdom. An enormous statue of the goddess—coated with gold and ivory—stood in an inner room.

The Acropolis in Athens represents the achievements of the ancient Greeks. Its stately structures were built in the 400's B.C., under the leadership of Pericles.

The early Greeks believed that gods and goddesses were always watching over them. They made offerings, held ceremonies, and attended religious festivals. Athletic competitions—in events such as javelin throwing and chariot racing—were often held at these festivals. In fact, today's Olympic Games are a modern version of a Greek festival that was held every four years to honor Zeus, king of all the gods.

A time known as the Golden Age took place in Athens between 477 and 431 B.C. The Parthenon, a magnificent Greek temple housing a statue of Athena, was built on the Acropolis during this period. Great plays were performed at religious festivals. Socrates and other philosophers explored and defined the nature of life. Advances were made in both art and science.

The Golden Age came to an end in 431 B.C., when Sparta, aided by the Persians, defeated Athens in the Peloponnesian War. The warfare continued into succeeding decades, as other Greek city-states unsuccessfully attempted to increase their power.

HISTORY & GOVERNMENT

In 338 B.C., the city-states of Greece were conquered by the Macedonians, who lived to the north. Soon afterwards, under the bold leadership of Alexander the Great, the Macedonians conquered the entire Persian Empire.

Alexander the Great died in 323 B.C., and his empire was divided. Greece, however, remained under Macedonian control until 146 B.C., when it was conquered by the Romans. The period between these two events is known as the Hellenistic Age. During this time, education was emphasized, new forms of literature were developed, and great advances were made in the sciences.

The Roman Emperor Hadrian built this arch around 132 A.D. It divided old Athens from the Roman city of Hadrianapolis.

A Greek Orthodox monastery is nestled among cypress trees on the tiny island of Pondiconissi, just off the larger island of Corfu. Christianity was spreading throughout Greece by the 300's A.D.

Beginning in the 300's A.D., Christianity—which was spreading through the Roman Empire—began to replace the gods and goddesses of traditional Greek religion. In 395 A.D., the Roman Empire was divided into two parts, East and West. Greece became a part of the Eastern Roman Empire, which survived until 1453, when it fell to the Ottoman Turks. The Turks practiced the religion of Islam, but they allowed the Greeks religious freedom and the chance to govern themselves. The Greeks, however, weren't satisfied with that. They rebelled against the Turks in 1821, and won their freedom in 1829.

Since then, the government of Greece has changed many times. Despite the democratic ideals of the ancient Greeks, Greece has often had undemocratic governments. In 1974, however, voters chose to make Greece a republic, rather than the monarchy it had been. Today, the people elect the 300 members of the parliament, or law-making body. The president is elected by the parliament. The prime minister is the leader of the political party with the most members in parliament.

AGRICULTURE & INDUSTRY

Agriculture in Greece has a long history of succeeding against the odds. Greek farmers must deal with rough land and rocky soil. Summers can be so dry that the rivers all but disappear. Many rural villages still don't have electricity. Even so, farming is a way of life for many Greek people. Nearly one-third of all Greek workers are engaged in agriculture.

In general, the best farmland is found along the seacoasts. Olive groves are a common sight in these regions. Olive trees are hardy and well-suited to the Mediterranean climate. In some areas, the trees are hundreds of years old! Greek farmers produce many different varieties of olives—big and small, smooth and wrinkled, green, black, or brown. Both olives and olive oil have an important place in Greek cuisine. Olive oil is also used as fuel in church lamps.

Olive trees stretch across the countryside in Peloponnesus, the peninsula that forms the southern part of the Greek mainland.

eep and other
stock are raised
reas that don't
port crops.

Besides olives, Greek farmers grow many other crops, such as grapes, lemons, cotton, wheat, and vegetables. Greece is a leading producer of figs and raisins. Tobacco is another big crop, and is an important export. Sheep, goats, and cattle are raised in areas where the terrain is too rugged, or the soil too poor, for cultivated crops. Greek farmers also raise a great deal of poultry.

Greece is not a major fishing country. Despite its 9,300 miles of coastline, only small fish, like sardines, mackerel, and anchovies, are caught in the Mediterranean Sea. Minerals are also in short supply, but do include bauxite, which is used to make aluminum, and lignite, a type of coal.

The Greek economy is still recovering from the disastrous effects of World War II, when Greece was occupied by the Germans and Italians. Industry is growing, however, and today employs about the same number of people as agriculture. Athens is the central industrial region, where products such as textiles, chemicals, metals, and cement are produced.

13

HOLIDAYS IN GREECE

The vast majority of Greeks (about 95 percent) belong to the Greek Orthodox Church, which is part of a larger organization called the Eastern Orthodox Churches. The Greek Orthodox Church is supported by government funds, and religion is taught in the public schools.

Most holidays, too, are connected with the church. Just about every village has a patron saint, and annual festivals are held in honor of that saint. The festivals include special foods, wine, folk music, and dancing. In some areas, colorful traditional clothing may be worn.

Easter is the most important holiday in Greece. The celebration begins on Good Friday, with people carrying lighted candles in the streets and churches. Midnight Mass is held on Saturday night. On Easter Sunday, many Greeks eat roasted lamb, cooked on a spit over hot coals. Other Easter foods are red-dyed eggs and sweet breads that are braided into fancy designs.

Musicians perform at pre-Lenten carnival in Pylos.

Roasted lamb is traditionally served on Easter Sunday.

New Year's Day, January 1, is called Saint Basil's Day in Greece. On this occasion, people give each other presents, and sprigs of basil are handed out as symbols of hospitality. A New Year's cake, called a *vasilopitta*, is served. It is baked with a coin inside it, and the person who receives the coin is said to have good luck for the coming year.

A few Greek customs relate more to the ancient Greek gods than to the Orthodox Church. In some towns in the areas of Macedonia and Thrace, for instance, the Greeks take part in a tradition that developed out of ancient fertility rites. Each year, on January 8, the women lock their husbands in the house to do chores! While the men work, the women go out drinking with their friends.

During the summer, many cities hold cultural festivals that celebrate Greek drama, art, literature, dance, and music. The Greeks also enjoy a great number of athletic competitions, fairs, and wine festivals.

15

FOOD CUSTOMS IN GREECE

The Greek legacy to the world includes more than magnificent ruins and myths—it includes food as well. As far back as the 400's B.C., a Greek named Archestrate became the first food critic, traveling throughout the Mediterranean region and writing an epic poem about the foods he discovered along the way. Today, Greek cooking is enjoyed throughout the world.

The cuisine of Greece was influenced by the Romans and the Turks—and vice versa. Geography and climate have also had an important role. Greece's rugged terrain is well-suited for grazing sheep and goats. As a result, lamb, mutton, cheese, and yogurt are common ingredients in Greek meals. Lemons and olives grow well in the hot, sunny weather of Greece. They are used often in Greek cooking, as are eggplants, artichokes, peppers, zucchini, and other fresh vegetables. Fish and seafood are other staples in the Greek diet.

Fresh peaches, tomatoes, and Greek salami make up this picnic meal.

A vendor sells green grapes on a street in Athens.

Native-grown herbs are used to season Greek food. Oregano is the most popular herb by far, but others that are used frequently include garlic, rosemary, spearmint, thyme, dill, anise, and cinnamon. Honey is commonly used as a sweetener.

The Orthodox Church has also influenced Greek cooking. Lent is a time of penitence that ends on Easter Sunday. During Lent, many Greeks go without meat. Therefore, soups and stews made from beans, vegetables, or seafood are served during this time.

In Greece, breakfast is usually a small meal. It may consist of fruit, bread, cheese, and coffee. In rural areas, especially, lunch is the biggest meal of the day. It is served around two o'clock, and is followed by an afternoon rest period. Businesses and schools shut down during this time, and reopen later in the afternoon. Dinner is served late, about ten o'clock. It is traditionally a time for families to get together and talk about the day's activities.

SOME GREEK SPECIALTIES

There are many delicious foods that are associated with Greece. One dish that has been served since ancient times is *dolmadés*, or stuffed grape leaves. It is a good example of how Greek cooking makes use of plentiful, inexpensive ingredients. Dolmadés are made by wrapping grape leaves around a filling of rice and seasoned ground beef or lamb. The stuffed leaves are then cooked in broth and lemon juice. During Lent, dolmadés may be made without meat.

Phyllo, a paper-thin pastry dough, is used in many Greek recipes. Sheets of phyllo may be wrapped around bits of crab, lamb, or chicken to make appetizers, or even main dishes. Phyllo is also used to make many Greek desserts. Of these, *baklava* is probably the most widely known. Baklava is made by layering phyllo dough with nuts and a sweet, honey-based syrup.

Baklava is a pastry made with phyllo.

Feta is a popular Greek cheese made from sheep's and goat's milk. It is salty and white, and crumbles easily. It is used in traditional Greek salads, which are made of lettuce, tomatoes, olives, and feta. The salads are seasoned with oregano, lemon juice, and olive oil. Feta is often served as an appetizer at Greek cafés. Another popular appetizer is *dsadsiki*. It is made from yogurt, cucumber, garlic, and perhaps a touch of mint.

Fish and seafood soups are often served in Greece. The most famous Greek soup, however, is called *avgolemono*. It is made by slowly adding hot chicken broth to a sauce of eggs and lemon juice.

In ancient Greek culture, Dionysus was the god of wine. Today, wine is still an enjoyable part of Greek life. *Retsina* is a distinctive Greek drink—and an old one! Long ago, the Greeks used to put pine resin in their wine in order to preserve it. Modern retsina is made the same way. *Ouzo* is another favorite among the Greeks. It is a colorless liquor that tastes like licorice.

19

A FESTIVE MEAL

Dolmades with Lemon Sauce
Country Salad
Cold Avgolemono Soup
Baked Lamb Chops
Stuffed Tomatoes
Baklava

Dolmades (stuffed grape leaves) are served as an appetizer in this meal, but they can also be served as a main course. Baklava can be purchased at most large bakeries or supermarkets.

Dolmades with Lemon Sauce
    25 canned grape leaves (16-ounce jar)
    1 pound ground beef or lamb
    2 tablespoons mint leaves
    1 1/2 large onions, chopped
    1 8-ounce can tomato sauce
    2 eggs, beaten
    salt and pepper to taste
    1/3 cup olive oil

Lemon Sauce:
    2 lemons
    2 eggs
    liquid from dolmades
    2/3 cup chicken broth

1. Rinse grape leaves three or four times in water.
2. Combine ground beef, mint, onions, eggs, tomato sauce, eggs, salt, and pepper in a bowl.
3. Place about a tablespoon of the mixture in the middle of each grape leaf. Fold in sides, then roll up.
4. Put oil in a large pan, and fill with dolmades. Cover with water and bring to a boil. Reduce heat and simmer for 30 minutes.
5. Drain liquid from dolmades into another saucepan. Add the chicken broth to liquid.
6. Beat the eggs, then slowly add the liquid to the eggs while beating. Pour sauce over dolmades and simmer 15 minutes. Serves 6–8.

ld Avgolemono Soup

Cold Avgolemono Soup

4 eggs
3 10^1/$_2$-ounce cans chicken rice soup
juice of 2 lemons
1 pint whipping cream

1. In a large bowl, beat the eggs well, then add the lemon juice a little at a time.
2. Heat the chicken rice soup in a large pan. Slowly add the soup to the egg mixture, beating well with a wire whisk.
3. Return mixture to the large pan and cook until thick. *Do not boil!* Refrigerate for 2 or more hours.
4. Just before serving, whip the cream and stir into the soup. Garnish with chopped parsley and thin slices of lemon. Serves 6–8.

Country Salad

2 cloves garlic, peeled
2 large heads romaine or Bibb lettuce
8 radishes, sliced
2 green peppers, sliced
2 red or white onions, sliced
2 tomatoes, cut in wedges
1/3 pound feta cheese
15–20 Greek or black olives
4 tablespoons lemon juice
salt and pepper to taste
2/3 cup olive oil

1. Rub garlic cloves on surface of salad bowl. Tear lettuce into bite-size pieces and put in bowl with vegetables and olives. Break feta cheese into small chunks and add to bowl.
2. Add lemon juice, salt, pepper, and olive oil. Toss well. Serves 8.

Baked Lamb Chops

Baked Lamb Chops with Feta Cheese

4–6 loin or shoulder lamb chops
pepper to taste
oregano to taste
2 cloves garlic, peeled and cut into slivers
4 1/2 tablespoons melted butter
juice of 1 lemon
1/2 pound feta cheese, sliced

1. Place each chop on a piece of aluminum foil (shiny side up) large enough to wrap chop completely. Season chops with pepper and oregano. Cut 2 or 3 small slits in each chop and insert the garlic.
2. Wrap chops in foil part way. Combine melted butter and lemon juice, and pour over chops. Place a slice of cheese on each chop and wrap tightly.
3. Place chops in pan and bake at 350° for about 2 hours. Serve chops in foil envelopes. Serves 4–6.

Stuffed Tomatoes

8 tomatoes
1 medium onion, chopped
1/4 pound butter
1/2 pound ground lamb or beef
1/2 cup uncooked rice
1 teaspoon minced mint
1 teaspoon minced dill
salt and pepper to taste
1/4 pound feta cheese
1/4 cup water

1. Slice the tops off the tomatoes and set aside. Remove pulp and seeds; reserve the pulp.
2. Sauté onion in butter. Add lamb or beef and cook for 5 minutes.
3. Add rice, mint, dill, reserved tomato pulp, salt, and pepper. Mix well.
4. Fill the tomatoes with the mixture and crumble feta cheese on top.
5. Replace tomato tops. Place in a casserole dish with 1/4 cup water. Cover and bake at 350° for 30 minutes. Serves 8.

A LENTEN MEAL

Marinated Celery
Fish Soup
Fresh Fruit and Cheeses

This Lenten meal features fish—you can use any kind of boneless fillet. The marinated celery serves as both a refreshing salad and a vegetable.

Marinated Celery

> 1 head of celery
> ¹/₂ cup olive oil
> juice of 1 large lemon
> 1 tablespoon fennel leaves, crumbled
> 1 teaspoon thyme
> 1 teaspoon parsley
> 1 bay leaf
> salt and pepper to taste
> ¹/₂ cup water
> 1 lemon, cut into wedges

1. Wash the celery. Slice into 1 ¹/₂ -inch pieces.
2. Mix the oil, lemon juice, fennel, thyme, parsley, bay leaf, salt, pepper, and water in a large saucepan. Bring this mixture to a boil. Add the celery and enough extra water to just cover the celery. Bring to a boil, then reduce heat.
3. Cover and simmer for 15 minutes, or until celery is tender, but still crisp. Do not overcook.
4. Remove from heat. Refrigerate for at least 4 hours. Serve in small dishes with a lemon wedge. Serves 6–8.

Fish Soup

4 small to medium fish fillets
salt and pepper to taste
2 quarts water
2 carrots, sliced
2 onions, sliced
2 stalks celery, sliced
1 16-ounce can tomatoes, drained and chopped
½ cup olive oil
4 tablespoons white or brown rice

1. Season fish with salt and pepper.
2. Put vegetables and water in large pot and bring to a boil.
3. Add fish, oil, and rice. Reduce heat and simmer for 30 minutes.
4. Carefully remove fish fillets into soup bowls, then divide soup into bowls. Garnish with lemon slices. Serves 4.

Fish Soup

A SUMMER MEAL

Summer Salad
Keftedes
Rice Pudding

Feta cheese tops this Greek salad, part of a quick-and-easy summer meal.

Summer Salad

> *2–3 tomatoes, cut in wedges*
> *1 cucumber, sliced*
> *1 onion, sliced*
> *2 green peppers, cut in rings*
> *1/2 cup olive oil*
> *3 tablespoons wine vinegar*
> *salt and pepper, to taste*
> *1/2 pound feta cheese*
> *20 black olives*
> *1 tablespoon minced parsley*

1. Place the tomato wedges, cucumber, onion, and peppers in a bowl or on a plate.
2. Combine the olive oil, vinegar, salt, and pepper. Pour over the salad.
3. Sprinkle with parsley, feta cheese, and olives. Serves 6–8.

Keftedes

1 cup bread crumbs
2 cups milk
1/4 cup minced onion
1/2 pound butter
1 pound ground beef
1 pound ground pork
2 eggs, well beaten
2 teaspoons salt
1/2 teaspoon ground allspice
2 teaspoons ground cinnamon

1. Soak bread crumbs in 1 cup of the milk for 10 minutes. Combine bread crumbs, onion, beef, and pork, mixing well. Add the egg, remaining milk, and spices. Mix well.
2. Roll into balls, using about 1 heaping tablespoon of meat per ball.
3. Melt the butter in a frying pan and brown the meatballs on all sides over medium heat. Cover and cook on low heat for about 30 minutes, or until done. Serves 6–8.

Rice Pudding

1/2 cup uncooked white rice
8 cups milk
1 tablespoon flour
1 cup sugar
2 eggs, beaten
1 teaspoon vanilla extract
ground cinnamon

1. Gently simmer the rice with 6 cups milk in a heavy saucepan for 20 minutes, stirring often.
2. In a large bowl, mix the flour and sugar together. Add the beaten eggs, 2 cups of milk, and vanilla extract. Mix well.
3. Slowly add this to the rice mixture and simmer until thickened, about 35 minutes. The rice will rise to the top when it's done.
4. Cool, sprinkle with cinnamon, and refrigerate. Serves 6–8.

AN EVERYDAY MEAL

Pitas Stuffed with Beef

Pitas—often called "pocket bread"—are a common food in the Mediterranean region. They may be eaten plain or used to make a meal in itself.

Pitas Stuffed with Beef

¹/₂ cup dry red wine, or cooking wine
4 tablespoons olive oil
2 cloves garlic, minced
¹/₂ teaspoon dried oregano
4 tablespoons wine vinegar
¹/₂ teaspoon pepper
1 pound beefsteak, cut in strips
2 tablespoons olive oil
4 pitas (pocket breads)
2 cups chopped lettuce
1 cup tomato, diced
1 peeled cucumber, diced
1 cup plain yogurt

1. Combine wine, oil, garlic, oregano, wine vinegar, and pepper to make marinade. Cut steak into strips 2 inches long by ¹/₄ inch wide. Marinate beef strips for 1–2 hours.
2. Heat oil in large frying pan. Drain meat and cook on high heat for 2–3 minutes, or until brown on all sides.
3. Prepare vegetables and put them in bowls. Do the same for the beef and yogurt. Slice the pitas in half. Allow each person to make his or her own sandwich. Serves 4.

GLOSSARY OF COOKING TERMS

For those readers who are less experienced in the kitchen, the following list explains the cooking terms used in this book.

Chopped	Cut into small pieces measuring about ½ inch thick. Finely chopped pieces should be about ⅛ inch thick.
Diced	Cut into small cubes.
Garnished	Decorated.
Grated	Cut into small pieces by using a grater.
Greased	Having been lightly coated with oil, butter, or margarine to prevent sticking.
Knead	To work dough with one's hands.
Marinate	To cover and soak with a mixture of juices, called a marinade.
Minced	Chopped into very tiny pieces.
Pinch	The amount you can pick up between your thumb and forefinger.
Reserve	To set aside an ingredient for future use.
Sauté	To cook food in oil, butter, or margarine at high temperature, while stirring constantly.
Shredded	Cut into lengths of 1–2 inches, about ¼ inch across. Finely shredded ingredients should be about ⅛ inch across.
Simmer	To cook on a stove at the lowest setting.
Sliced	Cut into thin slices that show the original shape of the object.
Toss	To mix the ingredients in a salad.
Whisk	To beat using a hand whisk or electric mixer.

GREEK COOKING

To make the recipes in this book, you will need the following equipment and ingredients, which may not be in your kitchen:

Feta cheese Available in most supermarkets and health-food stores.

Garlic Fresh garlic can be bought in supermarkets. Each bulb can be broken into sections called cloves. You have to remove the brittle skin around each clove before chopping it.

Grape leaves Canned grape leaves are now available in many large supermarkets. You can substitute cabbage leaves if you need to. Gently boil a head of cabbage and remove the leaves as they soften.

Greek olives These black olives are saltier and more wrinkled than regular black olives. Many supermarkets sell them. Substitute regular black olives if you can't find them.

Olive oil An oil made by pressing olives. It can be found in most supermarkets.

Orange marmalade This jam can be found at a supermarket.

Phyllo pastry This super-thin dough can be found in large supermarkets or imported-foods specialty stores. Most large cities will have Greek grocery stores.

Pitas Also called "pocket bread," pitas can be found in most supermarkets.

Spices Cinnamon, cloves, allspice, and vanilla extract will be found with other spices in a supermarket.

Olive trees are found all over the Greek countryside.

INDEX

We would like to thank and acknowledge the following people for the use of their photographs and transparencies:

Mark E. Ahlstrom: cover inset, 18, 21, 22, 25, 26, 28; Blue Seas Trading Company: 9, 10, 11; Classic Studies Department, Gustavus Adolphus College: cover, 2, 7, 8, 12, 13, 14, 15, 16, 17, 19, 30.

Produced by Mark E. Ahlstrom (The Bookworks)
Typesetting and layout by The Final Word
Photo research by Judith Ahlstrom